Turkeys In Disguise

Story by Jordan Macocha

Illustrations by Jordan Macocha

MOUNTAINS

TURKEY

TERRITORY

Once upon a time there lived a large family of turkeys.
Not too far away there was also a pilgrim village, and,
unfortunately, this caused a problem. Every Thanksgiving
the pilgrims would capture a group of turkeys and pluck
off their feathers for clothes and hats.

Instead of capturing the turkeys by hand, the pilgrims had a special weapon: a rope gun. This would tie-up the turkeys and reel them in to be taken to Pilgrim Town.

Knowing how much it will hurt to be plucked of their feathers, all of the turkeys were panicking, except one. His name was Tom, and he was a very smart turkey. While listening to his panicking friends, Tom came up with an idea.

Since tomorrow is Thanksgiving and the pilgrims will be coming soon, he decided it was time to share his plan with the rest of the turkeys. They were so scared they said they would try anything.

At first the turkeys were in shock at what Tom had made; they did not think it would work. They were not sure if a brown bag with a picture on it could fool the Pilgrims, and they thought Tom was crazy.

But then they heard the sound of the pilgrims coming. Their minds were made up: they would try Tom's idea, or lose their feathers.

When the turkeys heard the pilgrims coming, they all put on their disguises. They all looked and started acting like cows. As for the pilgrims, they were so confused that after about ten minutes, they finally went home. They did not know the turkeys were in disguises.

After the pilgrims left, all the turkeys celebrated their success, except Tom. Tom knew more people would come, and he needed more masks.

As for the pilgrims, they went straight home. After some thought they went to their neighbors, the farmers, and told them about all the cows they had seen. The farmers thanked the pilgrims, and both the pilgrims and the farmers set out to round up the newly found cows.

However, when the farmers and the pilgrims
arrived, they did not find cows, they found cats!
Both the farmers and the pilgrims were fooled.
As before, there was a long time of staring, and
then finally they all left.

After being fooled, the farmers went to their neighbors the dog trainers. The farmers and the pilgrims told them about the cats. They were very eager to catch them. This time the pilgrims, farmers, and dog trainers would all go to capture the new animals.

Knowing that the pilgrims and the
farmers would return with more people,
Tom thought up another disguise that would confuse
them so much that they would have to give up trying to capture them.

Just as Tom thought, the pilgrims, farmers,
and dog trainers were completely
unprepared for what they saw.

Pilgrims! Tom had made pilgrim masks and
their own rope guns! The pilgrims, farmers,
and dog trainers could not believe it! Instead of animals,
pilgrims were staring back at them. They were so
confused that they left without a peep.

Right after all the people had left, Tom was right back at work making new masks for the next time the pilgrims would return. However, after a long time of waiting, no one came; no pilgrims, farmers, or dog trainers.

Feeling that they had won for good, the turkeys partied late into the night like never before! Still, Tom had a bad feeling that something was going on in the pilgrim village. He needed to find out what! He had one last disguise up his feathers….

So, with a pair of spy sunglasses and a hat, Tom was off on an undercover mission to Pilgrim Town.

When Tom made it to the Root Beer House, where all the people of the town hung out, it was getting dark. Thanksgiving was coming fast, and he needed to find out what their plans were for the next day.

Tom walked in quietly to the largely empty space and sat at a table near the back of the room. As Tom sat there, he gathered information on their plans. He listened to the lead pilgrim as he talked: "Tomorrow we will go back to where we saw all the animals, and whatever is there, we are going to rope up and bring them back here. We will use their fur, hide, or feathers and wear them for Thanksgiving dinner!"

Hearing this, Tom was horrified, and he ran as fast as his turkey legs would take him. He had to relay the plans of the humans to his friends before it was too late.

By the time Tom reached his friends, he was so out of breath that he could not get the message out.... and Tom knew he did not have much time.

When Tom was finally able to speak,
he could already see images of many men on the horizon.
The pilgrims were HERE!

When the pilgrims, farmers, and dog trainers reached where the turkeys were hiding, all the turkeys were scattered throughout the area. They were hiding in trees and running everywhere. Tom even tried to make a new disguise, but the pilgrims stopped him by using their rope guns to take his supplies.

The attack only lasted a short time, but that is all it took to rope all the turkeys and get them ready to take back to Pilgrim Town. However, Tom was still free.

It was not long before the pilgrims cornered
Tom. Now all Tom had was his brain to save
him and his friends!!!

"Why do you pluck our feathers?" Tom asked, "Why can't we just get along?" Then the lead pilgrim answered, "We need your feathers to keep us warm in the winter. Anyway, your feathers grow back."

Hearing this, Tom came up with an idea. He said, "Well, we shed our feathers every year. If you show us kindness, caring, and compassion, we will give you our feathers. That way you do not have to try to capture us, and we do not get hurt. You can easily just pick them up once every year when we shed them and use them to make clothes to keep you warm. That way, everybody wins!"

The pilgrims agreed and liked the solution that
Tom came up with, and, in the end, the pilgrims
and the turkeys both signed a treaty to live in
peace with each other.

And they all lived happily ever after.

THE END

Questions:

How could you in your everyday life solve problems by thinking the situations through and making it work better for everyone?

Are you able to come up with some solutions to some problems or situations you have in your life?

Thank you for reading my book. I would also like to thank the following teachers who have encouraged my writing, unique ideas and have pushed me to publish my stories: Mrs. Bozynski, my second grade teacher, Mrs. Wittbold, my fifth grade teacher and Mrs. Dolsen, my sixth grade teacher.

Thank you to my family and especially my mom, whom without I would never have published my book; it would be under some papers in a box with my other school keepsakes and papers.

I worked many years on my book; redoing it many times to get it to be something that I hoped would be good, funny and have a moral to give everyone who read it some laughs and something to think about.

I am also giving a portion of the proceeds to charity so I can help **in my own way.**

Made in the USA
Las Vegas, NV
05 June 2024

90758935R00024